I am just like you!

BY KELLY SCRIVENER

Illustrations by Lynda W. Daddona

For my boys, who have made me so proud, showing friend[...]
and compassion to people with disabilities and treating the[...]
with respect. To my husband, who has supported me over the
many years with my passion for horses and helping people.
And to my mom, who encouraged me to do this book and shares
it with me in her artwork.

 **FriesenPress**

Suite 300 - 990 Fort St
Victoria, BC, Canada, V8V 3K2
www.friesenpress.com

ISBN
978-1-4602-6848-3 (Paperback)
978-1-4602-6849-0 (eBook)

1. Juvenile Nonfiction

Distributed to the trade by The Ingram Book Company

For my boys, who have made me so proud, showing friendship and compassion to people with disabilities and treating them with respect. To my husband, who has supported me over the many years with my passion for horses and helping people. And to my mom, who encouraged me to do this book and shares it with me in her artwork.

Friesen Press

Suite 300 - 990 Fort St
Victoria, BC, Canada, V8V 3K2
www.friesenpress.com

Copyright © 2015 by Kelly Scrivener
First Edition — 2015

Illustrations by Lynda W. Daddona

ISBN
978-1-4602-6848-3 (Paperback)
978-1-4602-6849-0 (eBook)

1. Juvenile Nonfiction

Distributed to the trade by The Ingram Book Company

I am just like you!

BY KELLY SCRIVENER

Illustrations by Lynda W. Daddona

I have *Cerebral Palsy*.

It makes my muscles tight and it is harder for me to walk. I use a paediatric walker, which helps me get around much easier.

Sometimes I need to use my wheelchair, but...

i am just like you!

Some kids stare at me and
make fun of me.

That really hurts my feelings.

I *wish* they knew I was born this way. I can't help it. Just like you might have been born with brown hair, curly hair or freckles.

It's just *who* you are.

I like to read books and play games on my iPad.

i am just like you!

I go *swimming* at the pool with
my brother Ethan.

I *love* to ride my special bike
that's made just for me.

My best friend is Ashley.

We colour pictures together and play with my dog Pepper.

On nice days, Ashley and I love to fly my kite at the park.

On Saturdays, my mom takes me to the barn, where I get to do a very *special* activity.

Can you guess what it is?

I ride my special *horse*
named Holly!

Riding a horse, helps relax my tight
muscles and makes my
body *stronger*.

We play lots of fun *games* on the horses. Like Red Light, Green Light and Simon Says. We also do exercises to help stretch and work our muscles.

Just like you do in *gym class!*

I have many friends in my riding class too. One is named *Jake*.

He rides Smokey.

Jake has *Autism*.

At school, he gets to wear *cool* headphones.

Jake doesn't like loud noises and *sometimes* he yells when he gets mad.

Just like sometimes *you* get mad and want to yell!

Jake knows *everything* about dinosaurs! He is really smart.

he is just like you!

All kids are *different*. Some of us have different coloured hair or skin.

Some of us are short, some are tall.

Some kids even *speak* a different language.

Our differences make us *special*.

But we do lots of things the same.
And that is why...

i am just like you!